This Book Belongs To:

Made in the USA
Columbia, SC
25 October 2021

47772159R00057